Secret Wounds

Richard M. Berlin

Winner of the John Ciardi Prize for Poetry
Selected by Gary Young

 **BkMk Press**
University of Missouri-Kansas City

Financial assistance for this project has been provided by
the Missouri Arts Council, a state agency.

Cover Art: "Blue" by Glenn Losack, www.glennlosackmd.com
Author Photo: Susanne King
Book design: Susan L. Schurman
Managing Editor: Ben Furnish
Associate Editor: Michelle Boisseau

BkMk Press wishes to thank Curtis Bauer, Lindsey Martin-Bowen,
Susan Cobin, Steve Gehrke, Karen I. Johnson, Megan Hardeman,
Elaine K. Lally, Pamela Rasch, Linda Rodriguez, Josh Zink,
and Linda D. Brennaman.

Printing: Sheridan Books

Library of Congress Cataloging-in-Publication Data

Berlin, Richard M.
Secret wounds / Richard M. Berlin.
    p. cm.
"Winner of the John Ciardi Prize for Poetry, selected by Gary Young."

Summary: "Richard Berlin's poetry collection explores, from a psychiatrist's
perspective, emotional territory of doctors' relationships with patients who
suffer physically and emotionally from cancer, dialysis, cardiac treatment,
etc., and their relationships to music, family, death, and human hearts;
through fears and triumphs that come as a result, he reveals these secret
wounds a physician endures"--Provided by publisher.

ISBN 978-1-886157-81-1 (pbk. : alk. paper)
1. Psychiatrists--Poetry. 2. Physician and patient--Poetry. I. Title.
   PS3602.E7578 S43 2011
   811'.6--dc23
                                        2011028290
This book is set in Bell Gothic and ITC Tiepolo fonts.

ACKNOWLEDGMENTS

Most of the poems in this volume first appeared in my column, "Poetry of the Times," a monthly feature of *Psychiatric Times*. Many thanks to Susan Kweskin, Managing Editor, and the staff of *Psychiatric Times* for their care in publishing the poems every month.

I would also like to thank the editors of the following publications:

Berkshire Medical Journal: "Remembering Your Smile"

Journal of the American Medical Association: "After Reading Music from Apartment 8"

Journal of Medical Humanities: "First Date"

Journal of Outsider Poetry: "Cutting Toenails," "The Cellist"

Nimrod International Journal: "Last Concert of the Summer" and "The Juggler"

"Teamwork," "Surgery Rotation," and "On Call, 3 A.M." were included in *Body Language: Poems of the Medical Training Experience*. Neeta Jain, Dagan Coppock, Stephanie Brown Clark, Editors, BOA Editions, Ltd, 2006

Additional thanks to my patients, and to everyone who contributed to the creation of this book: Renee Ashley, Roslyn Berlin, Daniel Berlin, Steve Bierman, Jack Coulehan, Robert Deluty, Denise Duhamel, Julie and Barney Edmonds, Ben Furnish, Michael Kronig, Glenn Losack, Jill Meredith, Peter Murphy, Susan Schurman, and Gary Young.

My wife Susanne King and I have been partners since the day we met at the Northwestern University Medical School bookstore. I thank her every day for her love and support.

And very special thanks to Barry Sternlieb.

Secret Wounds

15	Lay Down Sally
16	The Prophecy
18	How a Psychiatrist Writes a Poem
20	Interned
22	The Killer
23	A Headlong Act of Love
24	Teaching Rounds
25	The Harvest
26	Good Fathers
27	Touch
28	Teamwork
29	Surgery Rotation
30	On Call, 3 A.M.
31	Medical Education
32	Dr. Kildare
33	Fungo
34	After My Father Died
35	The Cellist
36	Women Without Eyebrows
37	After Reading *Music from Apartment 8*
38	Wounds
39	How the News Comes
40	What to Call Me
41	Doctor Jokes
43	Denial
44	Critters
45	Hero
47	First Patient
48	Show of Force
49	Rage
50	Intimidation
51	First Date
52	Dropping the Lamb
53	Angel
55	Expert Witness

56	Olivia's Overlook
57	Still Life with Monhegan Island Poppies
58	The Scientists
60	Einstein's Happiest Moment
61	Practicing My Scales
62	How a Psychiatrist Tells Time
63	How a Psychiatrist Parties
64	A Psychiatrist's Double Life
65	The Proposition
66	Whores
68	Bad Debts
70	Meditation in the Dentist's Chair
71	The Juggler
72	Message in a Bottle
73	Treating Paul Celan
74	Another Tanglewood Tale
75	Huitzilopochtli
76	Nursing Home Doctors
77	The Piercing
79	The Garden of Eden
80	Married Life
81	Women Medical Student Poetry Reading
82	Cutting Toenails
84	Note to Pablo Neruda
85	Random Thoughts While Reading the "News and Notes" Section of the *Berkshire Medical Journal*
86	All the Sad Doctors
87	Where Doctors Hide
88	End of Summer
89	Ficus Lyrata
90	Obituaries in a Medical School Magazine
91	Stanley Robbins' Bookshelf
92	A Psychiatrist's Guitar
94	Playing in the Band
95	If I Were a Painter
96	Occupational Hazards
98	Last Concert of the Summer

For me, to be a writer is to acknowledge the secret wounds that we carry inside us, wounds so secret that we ourselves are barely aware of them…

—Orhan Pamuk, from his Nobel Prize acceptance speech

When they ask me, as of late they frequently do, how I have for so many years continued an equal interest in medicine and the poem, I reply that they amount for me to nearly the same thing.

—William Carlos Williams

FOREWORD

The poems in Richard Berlin's *Secret Wounds* offer a revealing, insider's look at the world of medicine, but they also allow us to consider our own lives from the perspective of someone familiar with the inner workings of our bodies and our minds, someone conversant with the invisible but inexorable processes that bring on illness, decline, and death. These are the poems of a doctor, a healer who inhabits a world where death is no philosophical trope, but a profound, ever-present reality. Death gives this book an undeniable, perhaps inevitable, gravitas, but in these poems death is a companion as much as it is a fate to be feared, avoided or ignored. In one poem a patient jokes that dying is easier than learning to play the guitar because "you don't even need to practice."

Berlin's subject matter is inherently interesting—the countless movies and television medical dramas produced over the years attest to that. In fact, TV's Dr. Kildare is the subject of one of the most touching poems in the book. But it takes more than an interesting subject or a compelling story to make a good poem. Medical situations are essential to *Secret Wounds*, but if Richard Berlin had become a car mechanic instead of a doctor, one suspects we'd be reading poems about sprockets and wrenches instead of IV drips and suicide attempts. Medicine is not the excuse for these poems; it is simply their occasion.

The drama inherent in the ICU or the operating room makes the descriptions of medical situations attractive and alluring, but it doesn't necessarily guarantee a successful poem. Berlin's poems are sure, spare, and always open to the task of revealing the mysteries he is privy to. The condition of a patient, Berlin tells us, "is broadcast from every face," and a good doctor must learn to read the subtleties in an expression, a gesture, a wound; a good poet must do the same. These poems are unflinching meditations on mortality, and on the art of healing and of poetry. It is a potent mix. What makes Berlin's poems stand out in the mind is his compassion. He is not afraid to take instruction where it is given:

> So we struck out
> on our own
> and learned
> from our patients
> the lessons we needed
> to know.

He remembers a first patient the way one might remember a first lover, and his poems are imbued with a rare tenderness. The "smell of death" may be in his nostrils, but Berlin makes his rounds with "praise on my lips / for any healing the earth might offer."

In the poem "Good Fathers," Berlin salutes one of the mentors who initiated him into the fraternity of healers to which he belongs. His poems in honor of teachers, mentors, and fellow doctors are particularly touching, and he gratefully acknowledges the master/apprentice model that medicine and poetry share. Berlin belongs to a small brotherhood of doctors who write poems. William Carlos Williams is the tutelary spirit of all poet/physicians, and Berlin clearly identifies with the epigraph that he has chosen from Dr. Williams, who declares that medicine and poetry "amount for me to nearly the same thing." His poem for John Stone, another poet/physician celebrates the wonders of a world "where doctors can be poets." We feel the vertigo of his dual vocation when he admits he's been shunned by doctors who feared his "poems / that spilled the secrets of their love / and hate." The doctors in these poems are not infallible; they leave gauze in a patient's brain, and their misdiagnoses sometimes cost a life. Disarmingly humble, one suspects that Berlin is in fundamental agreement with a patient who complains, "Doctors! Such fools!"

Berlin traces his decision to become a doctor back to his own father's death, a death he could not prevent. It seems that his filial devotion, his desire to save a beloved parent, has been absorbed and transferred, first to his patients, and now to his readers. In "Women Medical Student Poetry Reading," Berlin gives us an insight into the "poetry of healing," whose power is strong enough to heal the healers. Near this volume's end, we learn that Berlin's daughter has started medical school. The good doctor wonders why she would follow him into such a difficult profession; no one who reads *Secret Wounds* will wonder at all.

     —Gary Young
      Final Judge
      John Ciardi Prize for Poetry

For Rachel,
my daughter and colleague

Lay Down Sally

He's dying on dialysis—
I've known him
since my first days as a doctor,

and now he wants to quit.
I've been called
to write the sentence

that says he understands
the meaning of "no."
Seated on the corner of his bed,

I test him with questions
until Clapton rocks the radio
picking "Lay Down Sally,"

and I drift off, thinking
this is one more riff I'll never master.
Though my white coat touches his gown,

he sees I'm gone and calls me back:
Remember when Clapton was God?
And we're in the days of Blind Faith,

comparing calluses on our fingertips
earned from playing "Layla,"
and we agree dying is easier

than learning guitar. *Yeah*, he laughs,
you don't even need to practice.
We talk music as he fades,

his soft breathing a gentle strum.
A nurse hangs the morphine.
I write my blue notes.

The Prophecy

—Ramsey, New Jersey, August, 1953

In my earliest memory,
my father and I rest

on a wide, flat stone
at the edge of a lily pond,

the air hazy and hot
behind my uncle's new house.

I smell mud and algae and smoke
from my father's Lucky Strikes

and watch the gray rings
he whispers to the sky.

Belly-up near shore
a dead carp rots in the heat,

iridescent green flies
buzzing the skin and eyes,

my father taking a long stick
and stirring the body.

Fifty years later,
I remember this scene

like Joseph foretelling the future:
that I would become a son

who loved his dying father
from the far end of a rock,

that I would become a doctor,
comfortable with decay

humming at his feet,
and that I was destined for a life

filled with death
and so much determined beauty.

How a Psychiatrist Writes a Poem

I begin by remembering
my hours as a patient
and Freud's "Fundamental Rule":

Say Whatever Comes to Mind,
which is the sound of brown leaves
skittering across the sidewalk

on this mild November day
and the smell of smoke
from fires burning in the fields.

Then I relax into my leather chair
and recall the details of this morning—
my wife curled below our down comforter,

her breasts still warm while I dressed,
the texture of walnut bread in my mouth,
the taste of Earl Grey tea.

This is the moment my therapist
would cross his legs, look into my eyes,
and wait for me to reveal something

more painful, closer to the heart,
and just to please him
I might report a few small agonies

from my trip to the session—a delay
for the bridge repair at Rawson Brook,
the red glow from my battery-failure light,

or the threat of anthrax reported on the radio.
I'd say, *Bioterror reminds me of my father's illness.*
And now that I'm talking about my father,

I can see my therapist move forward
in his chair and nod a bit faster,
which brings something to mind

I never thought to discuss—
last night's conversation with my mother
who told me she has a melanoma

on her thigh, the thigh I hugged
as a five year old when we shopped
in the aisles of the Grand Union.

I remember those moments
as the closest we ever shared—
the soft, smooth plain of skin,

her delicate gold ankle bracelet,
khaki shorts and Shalimar perfume.
Yes, psychotherapy always leads back

to mother. But before I can resolve
my Oedipal drama in therapy or this poem,
before I can make sense of the grief

I am just beginning to feel,
I hear my therapist say, *Time's up*,
and he stands and gazes outside,

the way I gaze out my office window right now,
noticing how the leaves still cling
to the oak before they let go.

Interned

When the year began, I thought I'd write a record,
late at night, after the scut-work and basic business
had been numbered in needlesticks. I would heal
my patients and fill a hundred notebooks before I'd rest,
and I would tell stories of how I kept cool under fire
of cardiac arrest, of how each drop of blood hit my coat,

about my fame for diagnosing horrors I would sugar-coat
for the patient, my graceful prose in the medical record
filling the interns and Attending with awe. But that was before fire
burned me the first day: twenty new admissions, the business
office calling with names of patients with insurance, the rest
stranded on gurneys, as if lying in the corridor could heal

a tumor or a heart that had failed too long. *Heal
the patients!* the Attending would shout, his starched white coat
a reminder I was just a peon. Clean-shaven, he had time to rest,
and he scorched every word I wrote in the record,
pimped me when I presented a case, because the business
of Academic Medicine is to learn your place in the pecking order. *Fire*

me! I thought, *Let him stay awake all night in the fire-
storm of the wards. Ask him to find a way to heal
the alcoholics and malingerers whose only business
is to stay warm through the winter without a coat.*
Who cared anymore about progress notes in the record?
All I wanted was a night without my beeper, to rest

for twelve solid hours without seeing blood, while the rest
of the interns worked up admissions and turfed each fire
to consultants, every slave so tired they'd forget to record
anything they did. And groggy me the next morning, working to heal
the moaning, puking, screaming patients who bled on my coat—
I wished they would die, wished I'd gone into my father's business,

managed his factory where no one would give me the business
if I nodded off during a midday meeting or tried to rest,
even in the bathroom, because the pager in my coat
pocket blasted when I peed, screwed up my aim, the fire
in my bloodshot eyes so ferocious I wondered if I could heal
anyone, anyone at all. A single cure would have been a record.

My business that year was to walk through fire
without sleep or rest, to hope, *Someday I will heal*.
The blood on my coat holds the clearest record.

The Killer

The poem is a capsule where we wrap up our punishable secrets.
—William Carlos Williams

She was old and fragile
and I was just an intern
charged with guiding her care,
her seeing-eye dog in a city hospital.
When I saw a pulse in her jugular vein
I pressed my stethoscope to her chest—
she inhaled and I heard crackles,
like static on a trooper's radio.

I guessed heart failure.
The answer was pneumonia.

Oh, I caught my error the next morning,
dripped in fluids and ampicillin,
but she'd been in bed one day too long,
the clot in her calf broken apart
and trapped in the lattice of her lungs.
I stood by her side, stunned
when her breathing stopped,
and I called the team, barked
orders at the code. And I felt
like a killer cornered on a dead-end street,
cops and canines closing in,
thinking confession, still holding my gun.

A Headlong Act of Love

—from a line by Pablo Neruda

It was a headlong act of love
when I kissed her. She was gone.
No one could have saved her.
The dialyzer hummed a little love song.

The way I kissed her (she was gone)
was a reflex, a hand to break my fall.
The dialyzer hummed a little love song.
No one saw us, the curtains were drawn.

It was a reflex, a hand to break my fall.
My mouth was on her lips!
No one saw us, the curtains were drawn.
I'm a man who doesn't take risks.
The corridor was quiet, it was close to dawn.

I closed my eyes, but not for long.
Her lips on mine felt soft and warm.
No one could have saved her.
She was dead. I sang her a song—
It was a headlong act of love.

Teaching Rounds

His hand is a farmer's hand,
nails outlined with crescents of black
earth, skin calloused, tough as a paw.
With one finger he traces the wound
we plowed from sternum to pubis,
flicks the sharp tips of snipped catgut.
We all know what was buried inside.
His movements remind me of an afternoon
on the bank of the Li River when
I stroked the gray bark of an ancient
banyan tree, the sound of water flowing
below me, the wind brushing a beat
in the bamboo leaves. When I come back
the patient is crying. Our Attending answers
a routine page, an excuse to leave.
In the corridor, he demands a confession:
Who peeled back his bandage?
Who let him look? It was the wind,
I want to say, And the river, but
I keep quiet, eyes on his scrubbed fingers.

The Harvest

He stands like a farmer with hired hands
ready to begin the reaping:
two blue eyes and a heart,
the smooth liver shining like a prize
on a butcher's tray, dirt-brown kidneys
that turn blood into gold; limbs for grafting,
Winesap to Smokehouse, Red Roman to Empire.
They toil in a sterile field, pack produce on ice
fast as death's freedom allows.

When they've tilled the grit worth saving,
he savors the moment like the last warm breeze
of summer, pulls out the irrigation,
piles tools for cleaning,
chatter rising like October crows,
a carcass emptied of all desire.
He notices the ache in his legs,
hot breath behind the mask, and he rests
a gloved hand on someone's shoulder
just long enough to stop his shaking.

Good Fathers

—for James Daniels, M.D. (1938-2001)

We were three men alone in a ward room
built for fifty, dust film on the floor,
Dr. Daniels and I, scrubbed and sterile,
gloved and gowned, standing behind the patient,
our only light drifting through the dirty
glass windows. I performed the prep—
Betadine soaked into a sponge, painting
orange circles on the patient's back,
the room filled with the scent of young wine
poured too soon from the cask.
Week after week we practiced
on anonymous blue collar vets,
everything ordered and routine until
that day Dr. Daniels pressed the needle deep
and failed to find the spot, four times, five,
finally giving up and passing it to me.
I can still see the angle of the shaft
when I pierced the patient's skin,
the sundial shadow it cast on his back,
gold droplets of spinal fluid dripping
into a sterile tube, the look Dr. Daniels
flashed me, just like my father's that day
he pulled over and handed me the keys.

Touch

I remember the first time my fingers
burrowed the swamp where belly joins leg
to feel an artery throb. I was so scared by the sweat
and scars I wanted to call in sick, wanted to call
my mother and cry. But when I finally learned
to feel everything, I became a psychiatrist
who touches nothing but a patient's hand
at the first meeting and the final good bye—
so different from the minister I watched tonight
at Confirmation, how he held the smooth curve
of each student's head with his jeweled fingers,
charged them with Holy Spirit, an open palm
pressed to a cheek, his touch so fearless, so certain.

Teamwork

I was just a student doing scut work
with my Senior Resident when the call came in—
an ER patient in shock and a Charge Nurse
who needed a diagnosis. He dropped
the phone and we both started running—
he smelled a ruptured triple A
and we knew that surgery, STAT,
was the only chance for a save.
We careened down fourteen flights,
the Senior barking our game plan,
and we arrived at a blue body gasping
through a face mask, a single IV
dripping like a bad faucet, the Charge Nurse
in the corner stroking her stethoscope
with an alcohol swab, relaxed as a woman
polishing a silver service for twelve.
I called the OR as the Senior strapped
the patient down and ordered the nurse
to pull the lines. But she just glared,
lifted the phone, and called her supervisor,
the Senior whirling like a samurai,
grabbing the IV bag, ripping down X rays,
releasing the brakes, and smashing
the cart through the swinging doors,
the treatment room behind us littered
with severed lines and plastic tubes,
the nurse's scream chasing us down the hall:
Fucking assholes! You fucking assholes!

Surgery Rotation

The last weak rays of sun
shine on the drab green chart room walls.
The evening staff has finished report,
and the wing quiets as night comes on,
our team reviewing the final tasks
on our 36-hour shift—
a dressing for a gangrenous toe,
X rays to read, IVs to start.
The surgeon opens an aluminum chart
with two hundred colored pages
clipped by a spring, pink for progress
notes, blue for vital signs, lab values
stapled in like tattered rags
on a scarecrow. He points the cold
metal at me like an accusation,
and lets it fall just before I get my grip.
I can still see it tumble
like a cannonball Galileo dropped
from the Leaning Tower,
and I can still hear it explode
on the linoleum floor,
pages scattered like straw in a thunderstorm.
But what I remember best is how hard
the floor felt against my knees,
the dust-balls in the corner,
the way no one moved
to help me pick up the pages,
the shined black leather of the surgeon's shoes.

On Call, 3 A.M.

After she pages me to pronounce him,
we pull the white sheet to his chin
in one quick movement, our eyes
on his, then locked on each other's.
We see what we want.
In the deserted call room
with its fresh linen and barren walls,
we smell each other in the darkness,
the sweat on our scrubs, antiseptic soap
on our fingers. We lick each other's salt
like deer, ready to run if our pagers call.
We can strip a body fast, our uniforms falling
to the linoleum floor. And we know
what pours from the sea of our bodies
will not be tested in the lab,
that our words will not be written in a chart,
though our movements are as practiced
as any surgical procedure. When we finish
and kiss and wash our hands clean,
we smooth the sheets and pull them tight.
We even make hospital corners.

Medical Education

What they taught
in school was not
what we needed,
and what we needed
(they said)
could not be conveyed.

So we struck out
on our own
and learned from our patients
the lessons we needed
to know:

how to break
bad news,
place our own comfort last,
and say nothing
when nothing more could be said.

And we returned
what they taught
to others
who learned
what we knew
was almost enough.

Dr. Kildare

Years ago, when I still believed
Dr. Kildare could cure my father,
I stayed awake past my bedtime

to learn to be a doctor. All I remember
now is Kildare falling for Yvette Mimieux,
a woman whose cancer he couldn't cure.

I didn't learn how to treat my father
in that episode, but I memorized
"The Tyger," which Kildare and Yvette

recited before the commercials.
At the end, Kildare crying,
his patient receding into the mist,

the camera closes in on her lips
whispering *Tyger! Tyger! burning bright...*
My father died a few years later.

No one recited poetry
when they called a code and cracked his body.
And I grew up and became a doctor,

even married one as beautiful as Yvette.
But Medicine hasn't made me handsome
like Kildare, and patients don't recite Blake,

though there has been a kind of poetry
that flutters like TV screens in the fifties,
all the images in shades of gray.

Fungo

He walked home where the path cut
through right field, a blazer hanging off
his arm like a loose bandage,
the smells of subway sweat
and leather soaked into his skin.
He'd wave to future baseball stars
deep in fantasy and finish his forced march home.

One August night, when haze and humidity
hung over New Jersey like a steamy dream,
he loosened his tie and asked if he could hit
a few fly balls, fungo. I'd never seen him play,
and when he picked up the bat and ball
in the wrong hands, I pulled the cap over my eyes
and wished he had kept on walking.

I'd like to tell you he found his range,
launched a long fly ball to deep right field,
that he backed us to the fence,
his arms synchronized with the bat,
the ball flying in perfect arcs through twilight air,
that we stopped when the last line
drive cleared the outfield fence.

But the truth doesn't matter here.
What is left are the memories
of thick August air and cricket buzz,
the pink glow of city lights on haze,
a ball field paved over now in black,
all the shame sons can feel for fathers,
and the way I walk through late summer,
the smell of his sweat under my arms.

After My Father Died

I left the hotel without a map,
lost as a star

in the mid-morning sky.
Orange blossoms fell,

their fragrance clinging to the air
like cologne on his collar.

A gypsy begged and whispered,
Your eyes contain sadness and light

and for a moment I forgot
his body in a hospital bed,

noticed each separate stone
in this fortified city

built over centuries
by a hundred thousand hands,

and stood alone with only two:
one to smooth grief

from the faces
of my patients,

the other to jab
this pen into paper

like a shovel
stabbing a grave.

The Cellist

When Verdi's *Requiem* ends
we gather our empty bottles
and unfinished loaves to carry them
back to our dew-covered car.
That's when I see a couple
I consulted with fifteen years ago,
stopped for a rest on the long walk
through the parking lot. I notice
her legs, mottled blue and streaked
with bright slashes of red,
as if an angry sunset
had been grafted to her calves.
And I remember her husband
filling her syringe with insulin,
his beard faded now to white.
Tonight their eyes meet
with the spirit of sacred music,
her body held between his legs
like a cello, one hand stroking her neck,
his arm curled around her waist.

Women Without Eyebrows

Head wrapped in a black Gucci scarf,
hairless in places we are born without hair,
her cough is the sound of stone scraping nerve.
I've known her so long I remember
when she cut her bangs in a long straight line,
and graceful eyebrows framed blue eyes.

Years ago, I stood before the Mona Lisa,
eyebrows erased for two hundred years,
her enigmatic eyes turned from contact.
Though they say the mystery is in the smile,
I could not explain her expression
without punctuation marks over her eyes.

I picture Mona Lisa as I try to read my patient,
eyebrows gone since chemo, her smile
a shaft of light through clouds, the frame
above her eyes unchanging. And I am awed
by the miracle she has survived so long,
the mystery she can smile at all.

After Reading *Music from Apartment 8*

—for John Stone, M.D.

When I started out in medicine,
before I married and before
I had written a single poem,
I read your poetry like a hiker
on a treacherous trail who finally
stops to rest and drink and admire
the view of snow-capped peaks.
Three decades later I imagine you,
ten years younger than my father
would be if bad genes, bad luck, and bad
doctoring hadn't killed him long ago.
Without a father to guide me north,
your poems were a compass
pointing toward a world
where doctors can be poets,
where the pulse of each line
begins with the heartbeat we hear
when we bend close to our patients.
I pray you, too, are drinking deep
from whatever stream brings you
to your knees, and I hope
you can hear my boots striding
behind yours, cracked from the heat,
covered with dust, both soles still strong.

Wounds

Each wound contains
its own beauty—

blunt trauma indigo
walled below pale blue eyes,

the gashed leg
filigreed with blood,

an abdomen scored
by a surgeon's blade

each layer yielding
with its own sigh,

the biopsy site healed
in a straight red line.

Each wound speaks
its own language,

every incision, slash,
cutdown and scar

in this hospital where
bruise is not a metaphor.

Here the body's art
conspires with destruction,

and violence surprises
with beauty so intense

the eyes of all beholders
must learn to be blind.

How the News Comes

It can come with a doctor's steady stare
or words blunt as a headstone.
The news is published in lab reports,
breaks when old men stand
and femurs crack like frozen branches.
Headlines are written by fingers on a lump,
by eyes reporting shapes in an X-ray shadow,
and with stained sentences of cells on slides.
Sometimes it comes on fruity breath,
jaundiced skin, or sheets soaked
with banners of bright red blood.
We read it when a priest appears
and the nurse leaves, when a wife begs
her wasted husband to eat, when friends stop
calling and children run away.
Most days, news rants loud and public
as a tuned-out politician,
but if we have the courage to look,
it is broadcast from every face,
a black script all reporters know
by heart.

What to Call Me

Call me doc and I'm an old codger
in a country store, a well-chewed cigar
in the corner of my mouth,
ready to declare the wonder of Epsom salt.

Call me doctor and I will itemize
your benefits, risks, and alternatives
distant and calm
as a man reading a timetable.

Call me Doctor Berlin and I will stretch
across the fissure of detachment
and approach you like a father
reaching for his grown child.

Call me Richard and the mirrors will vanish
from my eyes fast as alcohol from skin.
For there are days I'm not sure
what to call myself, in whose name I heal.

Doctor Jokes

A surgeon knows nothing and does everything.
An internist knows everything and does nothing.
A psychiatrist knows nothing and does nothing.
And a pathologist knows everything, but a day too late.

—an old joke

I think they're funniest just after surgery,
masks askew, sweaty scrubs, woozy after hours
on their feet and another missed lunch.
Yet they stride into the lounge like heroes,
the pale families gathered like old newspapers,
and announce for the whole crowd to hear: *We got it all.*
If you knew the stats, you'd get the joke.

Internist comedy needs fewer people
but a lot more props: blood tests, X rays,
magnetic resonance imaging, and bundles of reports,
like guys at the track trying to nail the daily double.
They like to look far in the abstract distance,
toward the vanishing point, before they go for the punch line:
Take this pill and we can run more tests next month.

Psychiatrists used to be mimes. They'd sit and nod
and knew twenty-seven nonverbal sounds like *hmmm*
and *uh-huh* to let you know they were listening.
They could mirror any expression and even stay awake
but didn't get funny until they copied the internists.
I crack right up when I hear them say *chemical imbalance.*

As for pathologists, they've always been into black humor,
down there in the morgue, cutting up bodies and weighing livers
before lunch. Brash as surgeons without patients to lose,
theirs is a drier, more literary wit, almost like Proust in their
love for detail: *Specimen labeled breast mass, 4 X 6 cm, pale gray...*

You don't think this is funny? Just try hanging out
at a hospital without a sense of humor.
Lean an elbow on a nurse's cart stranded in the hall
and listen to the chorus of *Help me! Help me!* rising
from every room. If you're serious and somber
and don't get the joke, stand quiet between the cries
and listen for a giggle. Death always gets the last laugh.

Denial

—In memory of Jordan Fieldman, M.D. (1965-2004)

Everyone worries if their doctor graduated
last in his class, but Jordan, brilliant Jordan,
finished first, dead at 39, now measured
as an ounce of ash in an old brass urn.

Ten years we begged him, ten
years of *No!* for surgery to save him,
and now we mourn with cymbals and drums,
praying his life held a sacred lesson.

But if I could take him back to our clinic, I would
tie his arms in his white coat's
sleeves like a straitjacket, roll his Harvard
diploma into a breathing tube, shove it down his throat,

and cut out the gut we all knew would kill him.
So what if he struggled? I'd live with my sin.

Critters

At the end of winter
squirrels and coons forage
at the wood line, the fox
bounces by with a blue jay in his grin,

and a possum on our plowed driveway
looks so pale my daughter believes
she's seen a ghost. This morning
a bobcat sits in the meadow

like an Egyptian statue,
the way I do with patients,
just another critter
with my hairless white coat

dragging on the ground,
two short legs raising me
high enough to see a hungry world.
And I make my muted calls,

run down whatever paths are cleared,
the smell of death in my nostrils,
praise on my lips
for any healing the earth might offer.

Hero

The fundamental act of medical care is assumption of responsibility.
—Francis D. Moore, M.D.

The Captain's call came at 30,000 feet,
a flight attendant's hand pressing
an oxygen mask to a woman's mouth, her eyes
rolled back, chin on chest, every crisis I've
seen flashing through my mind—hemorrhagic
shock, respiratory arrest, code blue,
as if thirty years had not flown by
and I was back in training, not yet a
psychiatrist who read "Management
of In-Flight Medical Emergencies"
a few weeks earlier and thought: *No way
will I ever volunteer to deal with that!*
But there I was, on automatic pilot,
asking for a blood pressure cuff, IV
lines, a defibrillator, connected
by air-phone to an ER doc in Pittsburgh,
my finger on an irregular carotid
pulse working to reach forty beats.
The details of treatment were simple—
believe me, you could have done it yourself,
yet all the passengers filed out saying, *Thank you!
We didn't know a doctor would still help
in an emergency.* But I was like the heroes
on the evening news declaring, *No big deal.
Just doing my job*, and meaning it,
even if we can't let ourselves believe
their modesty. By midlife and midcareer,
there have been countless times I've worked hard
without thanks from anyone, practiced
with dishonor, knowing I didn't know
enough, because to be a doctor means

a life of shame— for every complication,
missed diagnosis, treatment failure, or death,
that airsick, empty, sour, sinking sense,
we feel when responsibility gnaws
and we struggle against our helplessness
clothed only in white coats that have no wings.

First Patient

She was ghetto black,
me, suburban white,
both twenty-five, meeting
in a free clinic basement
miles from medical school.
She heard a voice,
a man's voice whispering
Whore, you're a whore,
and all I knew was
to listen as if she were rain,
nodding yes, yes,
wishing I knew the cure.
And the voice stopped
when she started Prolixin,
and by then I could hear
my own voice reveal
the mystery of my career.
Maybe she wasn't
my first patient,
but she was the first
I remember.

Show of Force

Late at night, reason is weak medicine
when someone has left you.
He'd downed a few drinks, enough to loosen
the sharp edge of rage on his pulse.
With blood on his hands and fumes
on his breath, I couldn't convince him to stay.

Richard Selzer tangled with a wilder man
and sutured his ear to a leather gurney,
but being neither surgeon nor strong man
I tried warm words and hot coffee.

When he readied to bolt,
I syringed four milligrams of lorazepam
and called six state troopers who hit
the door like heat from a burning barn,
and he wilted, curled, climbed on the cart
for a quiet ride to the locked unit.

Months later, we spot each other
down a hospital corridor.
He's in blue coveralls, me in my white coat.
When he clenches his fist
I walk the other way.

Rage

Almost midnight and pissed off at my partner
who left early again to rescue her drunk
driving husband, leaving me to work up
the OD who wants to leave against my orders.
Twenty hours into this shift, the patient
is the enemy, one more life and death
decision before the possibility of sleep.
I listen to a minute of her story,
the breakup, the drugs, and *Yes,* she feels fine,
and *No,* she will never do this again,
and *Please will you let me go home right now?*

The hours pass, her labs are normal,
the attending signs off, but somewhere
south of midnight she needs a physical
and all I want is to strangle her
with my stethoscope and smash her knees
with my reflex hammer. Oh, I try to be
professional and examine her by the book—
head and heart, breath sounds and breasts,
commanding her to sit up tall and let me
inspect their symmetry, my stare as hard
and humiliating as rage can achieve.
But she lets me look for as long as I want,
my hate and my love hanging inches apart.

Intimidation

He blocks the path between me and the door
with his body and the smell of gin,
his wife still dressed in a hospital johnny,
charcoal crust caked on her lips.
Like a thunderhead on a stifling afternoon
his voice rises and I grow quiet,
sweat beading under my arms.
He waves his fist at me for keeping her prisoner
in the hospital, then suddenly reaches
inside his jacket—I'm sure he's going for a gun.
I wish I could say I responded like a martial artist,
but I sat as still as a hijacked passenger
imagining the perfect black circle
pointed at my face, the explosion
of gray smoke, the smell of black powder,
and I could see the sharp margins
of the entrance wound, gray matter
splashed on the wall, my blood pooled
on the floor. But his hand shoots out
with a photo of them at the beach,
his nails scratching her sunburned shoulder:
She's coming home now.

First Date

The scar on her sternum is a zipper
opened once to reveal her heart,

the smooth arc of her breasts
untouched since the bypass

fifteen hundred nights ago.
His body lies beside hers

pale as skim milk
after radiation scoured

the wild cells
from his marrow.

Like lonely travelers who plan
to meet in a foreign city

they have shared their stories
on the web,

how their return from the dead
troubles friends

the way gypsies disturb tourists
with sad eyes and outstretched hands.

And tonight in an airport motel,
each reveals one last secret

like a prisoner
who rips a silver coin

from a coat's silk lining
to seal a sacred oath.

Dropping the Lamb

If you're alone in the kitchen and drop the lamb, you can always just pick it up. Who's going to know it? —Julia Child

Imagine a neurosurgeon in scrubs
hunched over a dead man's chart

writing loops and strands
of twisted prose

illegible as pasta
lying on a plate.

Imagine the quick snip of day-old sutures,
scalpel slicing a crust of blood,

the careful retraction of scalp and brain
to retrieve a wad of gauze

left behind like yesterday's paper
on the backseat of a bus.

And imagine the patient's brain stem
herniating through the foramen magnum

in less time than it takes lamb
to drop from counter to floor,

how suddenly the heart stops beating,
nothing left for a neurosurgeon to write

except a post-op note
to erase responsibility

the way Julia would wipe
lamb's blood off the kitchen floor.

Angel

—for Chun Li, who adopted Angel *as her American name*

If you want to find an angel
ride a bamboo raft down the Dragon River,
past the waterwheel and ancient banyan tree
to the earthen dam and five steps
carved into the riverbank
that lead to the old inn door.

You will know her by her laugh
which rhymes with the sounds of the river
and the braid of black hair
held with white ribbon.

She will be perched on the counter
like an ornament, and you will wonder
how she learned to speak English,
navigate the Internet, and answer the phone.

She will send you to the fishing village
where they kept her hidden
because she has no legs,
where her bones grew so brittle
they broke like rice stalks after the harvest.

When you return, you will talk
about Bill Clinton's visit to her home,
the fragrance of the local tea,
about America, McDonald's and KFC,
and the medications they gave her in LA
to keep her from breaking again.

And you will learn to love her
almost as much as her mother
who picks her up and carries her
to the river in a pink Nike backpack,
her Angel as light as a set of wings.

Expert Witness

I'm driving the Mass Pike west
just before sunset, blacktop cleared
of snow, the only car for miles
after a late April storm. The distant
silhouettes of bare trees line up
along the Berkshire hills like the stubble
of my three-day beard, and wild clouds
spin arcs of steel-bar-blue, Creedence
on the radio singing "Fortunate Son,"
me remembering my father
like I always do at dusk on the highway,
1954, riding shotgun in our new Olds-
mobile sedan on Route 1, traffic
streaming toward us from the glow
of New York City, my father warning
me that twilight and dawn are the most
dangerous times to drive. In a few days
I will listen for his voice again when
I turn around and drive east at sunrise,
rehearsing my testimony for the trial
of a drug dealer accused of murder.
Crazy or sane? they will ask me,
Life in a hospital ward or slow death
in a prison yard? The defendant's father
will be speeding down the Mass Pike, too,
the sun's glare filling our eyes with tears,
both of us driving blind.

Olivia's Overlook

All year long they gather on this outcrop
carved by wind and water into the flank
of Lenox Mountain. They arrive on foot,
on road bikes and air conditioned SUVs
for a chance to sip wine, smoke a joint,
or just sit on the long stone wall and look
for dragons in the clouds. On July 4th
crowds come for fireworks over the lake,
and in January, when the sun sets early,
they park and turn up the heat, seduced
by the sky's glitter and black party dress.
But a few make the climb with a plan
for suicide—Jim Beam and a bottle of Oxy,
a well-oiled shotgun or a length of rope,
the lucky ones making it to our ICU,
others lying there wounded or dead
when the sun comes up and ignites
a scene that can take your breath away.

Still Life with Monhegan Island Poppies

I remember their wild clusters
waved by sea breeze near the old inn door,
petals and pods exposed like skin
sun might lick with lust,
how I yearned for their beauty,
and the moment, like Rapunzel's father, I stole them.

Back home, I scattered seeds on injured earth,
and they spread on wind to the wood-line,
past the pond where herons preen.
Years later, old temptation has flown
over the mountain to grow unchecked
in the cracks of city sidewalks.

Today I arrange thin green stems
and purple-black flowers in a pewter vase
where they will live one more day
before blossoms fall like punishment.
And after composing my dying still life,
I stand in the garden with a sharpened blade,

eager to cut heads
multiplied beyond all desire,
their halved seed pods
shaped in perfect omegas,
death and life blooming mindless as HIV,
ready to flower on whatever island will sustain them.

The Scientists

It's late afternoon and I'm burned out
from three long evaluations with ghetto boys
who saw me as the Grand Inquisitor.
My last case sits in the recliner and stares
out the window. With a do-rag on his head,
FuBu sweats, and unlaced Timberland boots,
he looks like the kind of boy the neighbors fear
might climb through their window at 2 A.M.
I learn he's on too many meds,
and tell him my plan to taper them,
but he's more concerned with knowing
how each one works, their structures,
formulas, and chemical names.
He tells me he studies reproduction,
not in the rap music way,
but the internal workings of an egg
brushed by cilia down the fallopian tube.
And he asks where each egg goes
if it fails to be fertilized, can we discover the cells
in a woman's urine or does her body absorb them?
An hour later we have pages of diagrams—
synaptic clefts, details of the uterine wall,
the intricate feedback loops
that control the rhythm of a menstrual cycle.
By now I've lost track of time
with this boy who reminds me of myself
when I imagined becoming a doctor,
how I tried to answer the same questions
about birth, death, and the body,

and the way forty years have passed,
the beauty still intoxicating, the spirit
of the research like a child swimming
for the first time in the sea, awed
by the waves, the smell of the air,
the mouthful of water with its shock of salt.

Einstein's Happiest Moment

—for Susanne

Einstein's happiest moment
occurred when he realized
a falling man falling
beside a falling apple
could also be described
as an apple and a man at rest
while the world falls around them.

And my happiest moment
occurred when I realized
you were falling for me,
right down to the core, and the rest,
relatively speaking, has flown past
faster than the speed of light.

Practicing My Scales

When I learned my first scale at 45
I knew I would never rock out
like the pros who started as teenagers,
when time didn't matter and practicing
was just another form of play. While their
fingers spidered the fret board
I studied the music of Medicine, struggling
to find the melody in a patient's history,
to sing it to teachers who seemed to know
the score of every disease by heart.

Ten thousand patients later, I see
a woman for evaluation, and she asks
about my orientation—Freud, Jung,
psychopharmacolgy? And I play a riff,
a little tune that fits her story's minor key
but contains a few notes of hope.
And we both feel the rhythm
in my reply, seated in mirror images,
nodding together, keeping time.

How a Psychiatrist Tells Time

Once I told time in 50-minute hours
but now I measure months with poppies—

on the first of May, pale green buds break
the soil's thin clay crust. In June, wooly leaves

unfold and grow larger than my open
hand. Flower stalks rise like rocket trails

on the Fourth of July, blossoms explode
in pink petals fringed midnight-black, shimmer

three short days before they fall to earth.
By August, seed pods fill like Minoan urns,

their lids etched with twelve-pointed stars, each ray
a minute-hand on a numberless clock,

motionless, frozen in time by September's
first frost. Gray as driftwood, they broadcast

black seeds on October's quiet ground.
After Halloween I uproot brittle stalks

to mix them with wet, wormy compost.
And when I stand in the tilled November garden,

a million grains resting in the earth, time slows
with the smell of snow riding the northwest wind,

my patients still beside me, the flowered,
the withered, the dying, and the dead.

How a Psychiatrist Parties

—Archanes, Crete

At 4 A.M. I link arms and dance barefoot
with Nikos, Maria, and Georgio,
the lute and lyre mourning in a minor key,
the singer drunk with long-lost love.
We knock back shots of raki until dawn
when Georgio jumps to the center
or our circle, spreads his arms like heron wings,
leaps into the air and spins, the crowd
clapping time, smashing plates at his feet,
Nikos and Maria stomping on a tabletop.
And when the sun rises above the jagged
rim of Mt. Yiouhtas, I carry a folding chair
into the shade of an ancient olive tree
to watch the world twirl from a distance,
my toes curled into cool earth, leaves rattling,
the morning breeze blowing out the stars.

A Psychiatrist's Double Life

It is a joy to be hidden and a tragedy never to be discovered.
—D.W. Winicott

I've been thinking about my daughter
moving to China and about Li Po,
the T'ang Dynasty poet, who believed
his poems could cure malaria.
But for me, his words awaken
the sultry, malarial memories
of a man who lives a double life,
caught between the person I believed
myself to be and the image
the world could see—
a medical student
who wanted to be a doctor,
but not a real doctor, a psychiatrist,
yet not an ordinary psychiatrist,
but one who worked with patients
sick enough to need a kidney machine.
Then I became a doctor-poet
and my colleagues shunned me twice,
once out of fear I could read
their minds, and again for poems
that spilled the secrets of their love
and hate. Hidden, undiscovered,
if I wanted love and adoration,
this was no way to win it.

The Proposition

Years ago I wrote, *I love my patients,*
not as a group but one by one,
never thinking a time would come
when a patient would read my poem
back to me and offer her love.
But I had rehearsed my reply
many times: *Yes, strong feelings*
are part of treatment, and I am glad
you are telling me, though I was
already planning a consultation
with a colleague. And I was preparing
for her rage, wishing love could be
as simple as radioactive sugar
I've seen on lovers' PET scans,
glucose surging into cells,
the brain lit up in primary colors,
another hungry organ
determined to be satisfied.

Whores

When I raise my rates
he folds his fifty
dollar co-pay
and slides it up
my desk
like an enlisted man
on leave
easing a big
bill in a stripper's G-string.
He tells me
I'm like his war-
time whore
who loved him
on payday
and left
when his money
ran dry.
Each week
I lead him
in our dance,
excite him
with my offer
to listen to his dreams.
And I tell myself I do it
to ease his suffering,
because I get paid,
because I took an oath.
But every month,
when we devour
another round
of sessions,

I fill out forms
for insurance pimps
who won't pay
unless I reveal
the private parts.

Bad Debts

$240

47-year-old insurance salesman,
depressed, alcoholic, came in
eight times, once with his wife.
Stiffed me on the co-pays.
Lost his checkbook, forgot
his wallet. He liked to tell
stories, always the victim.
He was good at his work.
Sold me two months of BS.
And I bought it.

$1260

25-year-old sometime actress,
kept getting fired from day jobs.
Boyfriend beat her, stole her car.
She was pretty some days.
Wore too much lipstick,
smeared it on her
front teeth. Insurance paid
when she had it and she lied
when she didn't. Saw her off
and on for a couple of years.
She'd scream at me when
I'd ask her to pay. One day
she turned over two chairs
and fired me. I didn't take her
to collection.

$30

61-year-old entrepreneur, bad
diabetes. Did drugs, stopped,
survived a divorce, brightened up.
Then he loses a toe, another,
then his foot, his leg. Infection
lingers, terrible pain. Starts using.
Misses an appointment,
misses another. I call him.
No answer. A month goes by.
His son is on the phone.
Suicide. The note says *tell
the doc he was my best friend.
Tell him I'm sorry
I still owe him money.*

Meditation in the Dentist's Chair

I know this drill—
novocaine's sting, the smell of burnt
tooth, hands cradling my head
into position, the numb recognition
of fingers exploring my warm, wet,
mucosa. Over the years a thousand
patients have said that seeing me
is just like going to the dentist.
But I believe I'm tougher to take.
With me there is no anesthesia
or high-tech glue. No one leaves
my office with a gold crown
even if they yearn to be a prince.
The pills I prescribe don't fill cavities
in anyone's soul, and my bond
with patients is created from nothing
more substantial than empathy.
And I remind the few who love me
too much, that our first handshake
is the only time our flesh will touch,
no matter how great their hurt,
no matter how long it takes to heal.

The Juggler

The juggler's drum
loud with my heart's penny.
—Paul Celan

After he juggles three chainsaws and spins
twenty plates balanced on sticks, he moves
to the grand finale: ten Bowler hats tossed
across the arena and stacked on the ringmaster's
head. He gets to nine and misses, and misses
the tenth three more times, cheers rising
to a roar with each failure, until the drum
rolls and the spotlight finds him for the final
throw when he nails the last hat on top
of the stack and the audience stomps their praise.

Next morning, when I straighten my hat
it hits me: the misses were part of the act,
the juggler knowing the crowd would admire
his skill, but would love him even more for
his imperfections. And when I arrive
at my office, where there are no stage lights,
drum rolls, or applause, and the crowd
I work will only suffer more if I screw up,
I stand under my shingle juggling
the books and briefcases in my arms,
open the lock with a silver key,
and walk up the long flight of stairs,
head bowed, hat in hand.

Message in a Bottle

*The poem, being a manifestation of language and therefore essentially a dialogue,
can be a message inside a bottle, sent out in the not always secure belief that it
could be washed ashore somewhere, sometime, perhaps on a land of the heart...*
—Paul Celan

Whoever you are, I am writing to make contact,
to get my message to someone who will understand.
It is Friday, 7 P.M., and I've just finished my fifth
phone call to a managed-care automaton
in 800-Land, IV'd patient on an ER gurney,
and they've finally agreed to shell out for one hospital day.
Oh what a tedious victory! I refuse to condense
the world into 15-minute med-checks
or believe the myths of the medical model!
Read the titles on your bookshelf. They are the same
as mine. And tell me you believe the diagnosis
Disruptive Behavior Disorder, Not Otherwise Specified
is less imaginary than this poem, or the conceit
I am shipwrecked on a tropical island.
Please, I don't want to offend you, especially tonight
when my patient almost died and I feel helpless and alone.
I've made compromises, too. At times like this, I wish
I was Walt Whitman proclaiming my barbaric yawp
over the rooftops of the world. Yet I know I'm just a doctor
like you, whose tools are pills and listening and a certain
kind of love, and that you understand the loneliness of our work.
Walt would call you *comerado* but I will call you *colleague*,
and if you were here, I'd say, *Let's meet tonight at the red oak
on the Tanglewood lawn. Joshua Bell will be playing Beethoven,
and we can drink cold Spanish wine with curried scallops.
And when the concert ends and the crowd thins out, the stage
manager will turn down the lights, and we will look up
at the Milky Way, glowing like the edge of an infinite book,
the Big Dipper in the north pouring its sweet, distant light on all of us.*

Treating Paul Celan

They've healed me into pieces.
—Paul Celan

While considering Celan's suicide
I think back to Virginia Woolf drowning
herself and the psychiatrists who said
her soul was too sensitive to live
in an age filled with the madness of war,
though today we would call her *bipolar*
and say it was the weight of depression
that made her fill her woolen coat with rocks.

Paul Celan never made it to Bloomsbury,
never starred in a Merchant-Ivory film,
but I keep re-reading his "Death Fugue" poem
and wonder if he ever learned to savor
Parisian coffee and croissants after
the war, his father dead from typhus,
his mother with a Nazi bullet through her neck.

I daydream I'm treating him at the Salpêtrière,
my office window shaded by a plane tree,
Celan seated across from me describing
nightmares even an SSRI can't cure.
I imagine my diagnosis, the way I would listen,
my metaphors. But after we've met
for the time it takes to smoke eight hundred
packs of cigarettes, after all the medication trials,
the damaged sighs and side effects, I wonder,
Would Celan still drown himself in the River Seine?

Another Tanglewood Tale

One sultry summer night when the white pines
stood still and the orchestra played in shirtsleeves,
the cymbals crashed to end the symphony's
third movement, and a woman collapsed
on the lawn. After she opened her eyes
in the first-aid tent, a cardiologist
asked about her heart, an internist wondered
if she might be diabetic, and a neurologist
ventured she must have vertigo. But she waved
away their questions until a psychiatrist asked,
Why do you think you collapsed?
And she raised her blue eyes, measured each
physician like a maestro leading a children's orchestra:
Doctors! Such fools! It was the Ludwig van Beethoven!

Huitzilopochtli

I've heard it said that the best time to write
is when you have nothing to write about,
like this morning on Monhegan Island
gazing through a picture window at the gray
deck, a pair of green canvas chairs, treetops
waving in the ocean breeze, the misty
blue sea merging with a cloudless sky.
A hummingbird hovers at the rugosa rose,
and I wonder if this is Huitzilopochtli,
the Aztec war god whose name means
left-handed hummingbird,
which reminds me it was once illegal
to be left-handed in Albania.

The doctor in me loves these useless facts,
still aping professors who could rattle
off symptoms of a rare disease found
only in the mountains of Mexico.
But I hated those white-coated men
who shamed me with commands for details
they knew I didn't know. If only they had told me
theirs was the path of the academic warrior
trying to pump himself up from hummingbird
into hawk, I would have found a way to love
the bitter taste of their arrogance.
We might have sat sipping coffee
at a fourteenth-floor window, watching
red-tails ride thermals in the summer sky,
life circling with the cry of death in its mouth.

Nursing Home Doctors

After each lap around the circular hall
the aides smile, *Hello, Doctor!*
and he nods at their greetings
like a general inspecting his troops.
Dressed in the frayed polyester suit
I saw him wear on hospital rounds,
he cradles a baby-blue chart, and stops
at random doorways to review his records.
I say *good morning* and he studies me
in my white coat, like a skin lesion
he has seen only once in a textbook.
And I lead him to the door with a shingle
posted outside, his old oak desk
laid out with a blotter, fountain pen,
and a spoon for applesauce he eats
while he writes long, illegible reports,
falling asleep hours past midnight,
just as he did during forty years of practice,
in the arms of his worn-out leather chair.

The Piercing

—for Rachel

Belly exposed,
she lays on the table

hand in mine,
the room filled

with Betadine's sweet smell.
A tattooed woman

swabs a careful imitation
of sterile procedure,

clamps a small tongue
of flesh above the navel,

and aims beveled steel
like a compass needle

locked on north.
A single red bead rises—

transformed an instant later
by two silver balls

to mark the spot
that bound mother and daughter

when she entered this world
on shining steel forceps,

her wet body
glistening in the light.

And I recall
the first piercing

scream, the cord
cut from her mother,

how fast she found
a breast, and the moment

she focused on the room
and our faces,

her sharp edge of awareness
cutting reality into small bites

before blood began to dry
on the umbilical clamp.

The Garden of Eden

Today when the ground was no longer
too wet to work and the world was all lilac
perfume, I pulled my scuffle hoe hard

through the clay's crust and heard
the blade scrape metal and earth.
I believed the sound came from nothing

more than a buried beer can tab
I dropped while foraging through
lettuce and sugar peas last spring.

But what surfaced from the fresh manure
was my lost wedding band, buried for years
in earth that nurtures love-lies-bleeding,

a ring from a thirty-year marriage, rescued
from the filth of paradise, hosed off, shining,
my cracked fingernails caked with dirt.

Married Life

—Montestigliano, Italy

No telling how many summers
have passed since the first stones
were hauled and set to build the villa.

No telling how many hooves and wheels
have gripped this hill and worked
the silver-green olive groves.

No telling the ages of the seasoned
couple who work this land,
their voices raised in an old argument,

the man bent and leaning on his shovel
like a crutch, the woman erect,
a seed basket in her leathery left hand,

the right wed to a machete,
raised high, slicing the Tuscan sun.

Women Medical Student Poetry Reading

They read sonnets for patients
who died before they could say
goodbye, sestinas about apricots
and elephants, and odes to anxiety
beginners must master. Virgins
in their experience with death
certificates, insurance forms,
and the power of money,
they want nothing more
than the chance to change
the world, one patient at a time.
In their gaze I see my wife's
green eyes the day we met,
kneeled on the bookstore floor,
the idealism she practiced
even when Medicine frayed her
like the cuffs of her first white coat.
And if there is a poetry of healing,
women, fearless in their show of love,
have taught me more than men.

Cutting Toenails

After I slipped
my finger inside and felt
death's rough stone
I knew I should grant
the old man's wish:
Just cut my toenails.
Down on my knees
I admired them, thick
as a silver dollar,
long and curved as
the shofar, the ram's horn
Jews blow on judgment day.
And I was dressed in white
like Yeshua, Jesus, my favorite
Jew, a healer I knew
would have been down
on his knees with me,
worshipping the beauty
of an old man's body.

I filled a vessel
with warm water,
soaked the nails soft,
washed the cracked
and calloused flesh,
and with my surgical steel
scissors cut sharp brown
crescents, like slivers
of a harvest moon,
imagining Yeshua,
what he atoned for
on Yom Kippur,
what pain he felt

for people he had not healed,
the expression in his eyes
when he heard the shofar's song
flying toward heaven.

Note to Pablo Neruda

I wake to dawn's pink light and palm warblers
twitching their tails as they feed in the pines
and I recall your line: *I was only*
a tunnel. The birds fled from me. I pull
your book from the shelf, study your picture—
a middle-aged man wearing a white shirt
and British cap, hands clasped, warm, sad, knowing
eyes looking into mine. I hear you ask,
Do birds fly from you, too? And I answer,
Long ago, when I became a doctor
I heard the sounds of pheasants drumming
in our chests, studied our eggs, our courtship
flight, the paper and nails we use to build
our nests, the long fall before we hit the ground.
My first patients gathered like winter song-
birds with their hungers and their fears, and late
at night I would read your poems, flowing
like an infinite black river, your words
carrying me high as crows when they harvest
morning stars in the heavens of their beaks.

Random Thoughts While Reading the "News and Notes" Section of the *Berkshire Medical Journal*

I arrived in town twenty years ago
with my doctor-wife nursing
our daughter, a fellowship diploma
and five publications notched in my CV,
my name in "News and Notes"
like the newcomers I read about now—
an anesthesiologist from Harvard,
a Phi Beta Kappa ER doc,
and a family medicine rookie
who knows about knees.
Oh, I understand their need
to convince us of their competence—
we were all just as insecure.
But if I wrote my blurb today,
I wouldn't advertise the length
of my CV or my academic rank.
I'd tell a joke I heard this morning
at the bedside of a dying man
I've known for twenty years,
how we sat holding hands,
the punch-line that made us laugh,
the one about how pathologists
know everything a day too late.

All the Sad Doctors

With black bags stuffed
below their eyes,
all the sad doctors
come to me now
like mourners
in the time of plague.
Crying in their office
bathrooms, carrying boxes
of charts home at night,
they are too tired to eat,
and sex excites them
less than a committee meeting.
Without dreams,
their eyes watch the clock
tick off
the wounded hours—
thousands of doctors writhing
on the scarred suture line
of American medicine
like a cargo of used syringes
washed up
with drowned birds
on an oil-soaked beach.

Where Doctors Hide

When a patient dies
and my pager goes off,
and a nurse brings in
a family member
who needs to talk,
and my pager cries again,
my heart rate jumping
to 120, my skin twitching
like a racehorse,
I hide in a fifth floor bathroom
no larger than a closet
with an old toilet,
rust-stained sink,
and a mirror the size of my face.
I look myself in the eye
to be sure my pupils
are equal and react to light,
measure my pulse
until the beat begins to slow,
run cold water on my wrists,
stuff paper towels under my arms,
hold cool compresses
to my forehead.
And I turn off the pager
and think about my colleagues,
who stand here
believing no one else knows
where they hide.

End of Summer

Pink anemones at my feet nod
and wave in the southern breeze.
Monarchs spread their wings
on an Adirondack chair while
I fill my mouth with raspberries
picked from our heavy canes.
A *New Yorker* story I'm reading
describes a 23-year-old soldier
in Iraq killed when shrapnel
smashed his skull just below
the helmet line, his parents
back home, grieving, my own
daughter, exactly his age
ribbon-dancing in China,
her biggest risk being run over
by a Shanghai taxi. And I'm
like the bluebirds, feasting
on ripe fruit before their journey
south, summer's last sweet taste
filling my mouth, staining my
fingers red as I ask myself how
I can complain about billing rates
and medical bureaucracy,
how I dare to complain
about anything, anything at all.

Ficus Lyrata

One September morning,
the day I started medical school,
I placed a two-foot specimen
in my sunny south window.
Then Chicago froze into fall
and reams of lecture notes
swelled into huge white drifts,
the heart-shaped ficus leaves
dropping like sad notes from
a Spanish song, and by finals
nothing remained except
rough brown scars
on cracked dead stems.

Today, on her own
September morning, my
daughter starts medical school
while I scratch my bald head
and wonder why she chose
to follow my old ambition.
And I wish I knew the way
to protect her from the avalanche
of facts and nights on call,
but all I can do is ramble around
the house, checking our plants
for aphids, feeding them
all the Miracle Grow I can find.

Obituaries in a Medical School Magazine

The section begins with a photograph
of a *Brain Surgeon/Banker* who died
in old age from miliary TB.   Back to
the Class of '36, each doctor's cause
of death is detailed with a pathologist's
precision—myeloproliferative disease,
interstitial pneumonitis, gout, the text
so different from the obits in our
local paper, where people always *pass*
after a *brief illness*. No, our doctor
tribe wants data: we know where babies
come from and where the echo of their
first scream ends. And we believe
the particulars of our own lives will lead
to different outcomes.
                              My eyes drift
back to the *Brain Surgeon/Banker's* face,
nothing like the usual portrait of Death
cloaked in a black cape and clutching
his scythe. This time he sports a starched
white coat, stethoscope folded in his hand,
and a Parker pen's arrow-clip attached to
his collar like Einstein's in the famous photo.
His eyes are rimmed with laugh lines, lips
sealed yet turned up in a gentle smile,
a face so warm and kind he could be
a colleague looking for new patients.
Call me, he seems to be saying,
I can make room in my schedule for you.

Stanley Robbins' Bookshelf

—for Stanley L. Robbins, M.D., 1915-2003

The words of a dead man
Are modified in the guts of the living.
          —W.H. Auden

If I were still a medical student
I'd tell Auden that Robbins' textbook taught me
our guts are folds of villi lined with
columnar epithelium. I'd be seated
on a royal-blue sofa with a broken spring,
light bleeding in just past sunset,
the room filled with smells of mahogany
and dust, Robbins' *Textbook of Pathology*
like a concrete block on my lap, his descriptions
of lesions packed into paragraphs like poems.
Back then I never pictured Stanley Robbins
as a writer, struggling to place the best
words in the best order, and I didn't know
his bookshelves were lined with Ginsberg,
Whitman, histology, and Plath.
As a student, all I felt was pressure
to learn the terms for ten thousand diseases
in five short months, their names a sacred text
that held the poetry of Medicine
I would recite some day to my patients,
like a love poem I knew by heart.

A Psychiatrist's Guitar

Hear the story of wood,
cut and stained

and carved for someone's need.
Caress the smooth neck

a palm can praise.
Smell mahogany

shaved and steamed,
fragrant as cinnamon.

Rake, slide, bend
tense strings,

make them breathe
each note.

Follow silver steel
over the bridge

from body to head,
each cord vibrating

when skilled hands
and calloused fingertips

pick sweet equations
where practice becomes song.

Listen for a minor key,
all the patience and flesh

in the finish,
like a man

in my office
composing a life.

Playing in the Band

All over this moonlit mountain neighbors call
the cops, and the cops call *TURN IT DOWN*,
but it's too late to stop "Wild Night"
with a hundred people dancing so hard
they've thrown off their shoes.
I'm turning fifty with a starburst
guitar hanging on my hips,
rhythm hand keyed to the hi-hat cymbal,
and when Billy rakes *E-D-A* and sings
Let me tell you 'bout my baby,
we crank it up another notch,
sweat pouring, wine pouring,
fireflies flashing like a marquee,
Billy belting out *G-L-O-R-I-A, Gloria!*,
his hair grown back from chemo, a glory,
my stepfather, on vacation from chemo, a glory,
Steven, smiling, one day post-chemo, a glory,
James in his tux, finished with chemo, a glory,
Marlena and my mother dancing
without their breasts, a glory,
all of us shimmering in summer's halo,
bandaged by rags of music and moonlight,
playing in this glorious band of the living,
shaking in time to our lives.

If I Were a Painter

—for Susanne

I would paint you the indigo band of blue
on the horizon, the slick strands of kelp
floating in the cove, lichen on the rocks,
lovage in the seaside garden, and sunlight
at dawn glinting off a gull's white back.
If I were a painter you might love me
like the night the terns gathered in the bay
and the sun set through a sea of coral clouds.
I would paint over the days I hurt you,
though I know you would say there is nothing
more I can do to color your love for me,
our marriage like an oil-on-canvas, nailed
to an outside wall, the frame warped by sun
and rain, the colors still vibrant, still true.

Occupational Hazards

Needle sticks and night call,
Hep B burrowing skin,
bad smells, deep wounds,
death, dying, dead wood
at committee meetings,
downward mobility,
delinquent dictations,
Medicare audits, M&M
conference, ombudsmen,
bureaucrats, fucking
bureaucrats, disease advocates
stretching my day
an hour past dark—
but these are nothing
compared to the dismal,
distorted lens
Medicine clamps on
our eyes, the vision
of life as disaster—
motorcycles as donor devices,
rock music and hearing loss,
sunshine and skin cancer,
deer and Lyme disease,
ice cream and steak
just preludes to the CCU.
And sex, well, pick your
nightmare from the list
of pleasures.
So what do I do?
Fish oil and aspirin,
sunscreen, a bicycle
helmet, buckle my seat belt,
and when I relax enough

to forget all the dangers
I ride my mountain bike
down a rocky trail,
maybe crank the volume
on my guitar, turn up
the distortion, or just
sit on a teak bench
beside the garden
to watch crows gather
in the branches of an old oak
and listen to alarm calls
that have nothing to do
with me.

Last Concert of the Summer

The moon comes up like a melody
from a sad old love song. On stage,
the orchestra plays a Mozart concerto,
summer slowing down on the last weekend
before the world goes back to work.
This has been a season of sick friends—
heart attacks, Hodgkin's, MS, and cancer
all scraping their one-note symphonies.
But saddest of all has been the young man
I've known since birth, who sees conspiracy
in the stars and the moon's jaundiced eye,
the medicines of our trade and Mozart's
triumphant music too weak to cure him.
The white-robed conductor waves his wand
and sways like a dancer at the crescendo,
me in the back row picturing the way
I place a stethoscope in my ears and listen
to the heart when I've run out of things to say.

Richard M. Berlin received his undergraduate and medical education at Northwestern University. The winner of numerous poetry awards, his first collection of poems *How JFK Killed My Father* won the Pearl Poetry Prize. He is also the author of two poetry chapbooks, *Code Blue* and *The Prophecy*. Berlin's poetry has appeared widely in anthologies and such journals as *Nimrod*, *JAMA*, and *The Lancet*. His column "Poetry of the Times" has appeared for more than ten years in *Psychiatric Times*. He has established the Gerald F. Berlin Creative Writing Prize (named for his father) for medical students, nursing students, and resident physicians at the University of Massachusetts Medical School, where the author is a senior affiliate in psychiatry. He has published more than sixty scientific papers and has edited *Sleep Disorders in Psychiatric Practice* and *Poets on Prozac: Mental Illness, Treatment, and the Creative Process*. He practices psychiatry in a small town in the Berkshire hills of western Massachusetts. His website is www.richardmberlin.com

Previous winners of the John Ciardi Prize for Poetry:

Mapmaking by Megan Harlan, selected by Sidney Wade
Tongue of War by Tony Barnstone, selected by B.H. Fairchild
Black Tupelo Country by Doug Ramspeck, selected by Leslie Adrienne Miller
Airs & Voices by Paula Bonnell, selected by Mark Jarman
Wayne's College of Beauty by David Swanger, selected by Colleen J. McElroy
The Portable Famine by Rane Arroyo, selected by Robin Becker
Fence Line by Curtis Bauer, selected by Christopher Buckley
Escape Artist by Terry Blackhawk, selected by Molly Peacock
Kentucky Swami by Tim Skeen, selected by Michael Burns
The Resurrection Machine by Steve Gehrke, selected by Miller Williams.